AFTERLIFE

WISCONSIN POETRY SERIES

Sean Bishop and Jesse Lee Kercheval, series editors

Ronald Wallace, founding series editor

AFTERLIFE

MICHAEL DHYNE

The University of Wisconsin Press

Publication of this book has been made possible, in part, through support
from the Brittingham Trust.

The University of Wisconsin Press
728 State Street, Suite 443
Madison, Wisconsin 53706
uwpress.wisc.edu

Gray's Inn House, 127 Clerkenwell Road
London EC1R 5DB, United Kingdom
eurospanbookstore.com

Printed in the United States of America
This book may be available in a digital edition.

Library of Congress Cataloging-in-Publication Data

Names: Dhyne, Michael, author.
Title: Afterlife / Michael Dhyne.
Other titles: Wisconsin poetry series.
Description: Madison, Wisconsin : The University of Wisconsin Press, 2023.
| Series: Wisconsin poetry series
Identifiers: LCCN 2023015001 | ISBN 9780299346843 (paperback)
Subjects: LCGFT: Poetry.
Classification: LCC PS3604.H96 A68 2023 | DDC 811/.6—dc23/eng/20230607
LC record available at https://lccn.loc.gov/2023015001

for my parents

I could almost hear . . . no, I could only imagine hearing it. And that
Is what it has become:
Having to imagine, having to imagine everything,
                    In detail, & without end.

—LARRY LEVIS

CONTENTS

AFTERLIFE

TO MY FATHER, THE LIGHT

In the room, there are two reels projecting onto the wall. One is playing
  your death and the other

my birth. One starts in a bathtub, the other staring up at the sky. Both
  in a pool of light—

of water, of blood, voices flickering on the soft flame of my ear. One starts
  with Mother

holding me up for your embrace, light passing through us thin as a blade.
  One starts

with your eyes closing, then opening for the last time, planes disappearing
  above you.

One starts with nothing, and one ends with it—cries like empty vowels
  shot through the air.

Where else could I go but deeper? The light pours over my hands
  like a wave.

I'm at the shore, your ashes on my fingers, your hands through my hair.
 The light

cuts through my chest and I'm blown open. It spills out like your blood
 on the tarmac,

the first time I made love. The reels catch fire. I try to save myself,

leaning against the wall as your image dissolves beside me. I can't see you,

only the light you passed through to get here.

KARA

We lifted the parachute
high as we could, took turns
on our backs, arms pulling the sky apart
overhead. Someone said
close your eyes and I felt the room
breathe. My father was there
and the house was on fire. We walked
the seam between rooms together
like I too had died and death
was a hallway. How else could I be there?
It was the dream we all had, our hands
becoming hands as we moved them
in tandem. He opened a door
and I couldn't tell the living
from the dead. I thought we all
were ascending. On the night my heart
finally opened, I saw a black ocean
hang like a pendulum under a black sky.
I swear I've never felt love like this.
I say I'm afraid I won't be the same
as I was before, and you say
it doesn't matter. Let go.

7

INSOMNIA

1

If memory starts at birth
I was born on the back stairs

as you wrapped your arms around me
saying   it was better this way

for him at least   that it was
instant   meaning

it didn't hurt   meaning
your father didn't know he was dying

Even now   the words leave
your mouth like hands

slipping from a table   Memory
trails off   becomes

what we need it to be—
silence   rowing out in waves

becoming touch

2

Barely sleeping. The bed
    an altar I waited in and the window beside it
the reflection that became the body,
    dreaming. Mother, what was I before this?

Each night I'd ask you what to think about, my hands
    reaching for his shape
in the dark. I'd hang my clothes from the door
    like I was dressing his ghost,

like I could see my past lit up
    before me—his eyes bright with my blood.
I knew where my imagination could take me,
    so I tried to exhaust it. Remember

the summer I'd stay up till the sun's first light, lacing
    my shoes in the dark? Those mornings,
I'd run along the overpass to the Bay, watching the planes
    land, slipping into the horizon just now

opening. In the picture of us before I knew
    what death was, he's holding my hand

on that small beach. I see the runway turning in the sky
    behind us, the tarmac

glimmering in the distance
    like the surface of the water.

3

          Where are you, my beloved?

                        [   ]

             I am right here.

AFTERLIFE

I'm in San Francisco again, in the basement of that big, pink church on the corner of 14th and Judah, handing Max a scrap of paper with the word *heaven* scrawled in cursive. Music is vibrating from the patchwork carpet like a prayer on fire, the reds, oranges, and yellows matching the sweet flame of his cheeks, as he steps out in front of us, conducting the other children from atop a piano bench, waving at empty spaces as if something were really there, something we can't see. And so they begin to act out his drama, what he needs to be real. Running around the room in silent fury, beating their bodies together, as if they could feel their lives unraveling—they pretend to kill each other, not knowing what their hands could do if they pressed them hard enough in the right places. But these kids don't understand death, thank god, or their own bodies. These kids whose mothers and fathers jumped from the Golden Gate or died of cancer or a brain aneurysm. Sometimes they don't even know what happened. One morning, Max's father just didn't wake up. And now, there's a room full of children playing dead on the floor, so Max comes down from his throne and touches each one of them, the newly dead, and they rise one at a time and begin to spiral around the room like little angels, whirling around me. I didn't know this could happen, that there's a place where I can see myself as I once was. In a room full of children with no mothers or fathers, dancing, I mean really dancing, in the basement of St. Anne's of the Sunset, in San Francisco, on a Wednesday night.

11

LIVING ROOM

I wish there was another way
to remember this, but grief has rendered

my past illegible—your blood
flowering the tarmac, my name

falling through a body
without form. What's left for me to hold?

A pile of ash? An image of you
that can't get any older?

When I tell people, *It was Father's Day*,
I always laugh a little, because it's a joke—

it has to be. Then I remember
the night before. All of us

on the couch in the living room
laughing about god knows what.

And I think, if I try really hard,
I can live in this moment

forever. I say, *Dad, tell me a story*,
and you tell me about the first time

you and Mom made love.
How it didn't feel so different

from the way you feel now.
How you could feel along her ribs

your own death, as if something inside her
might open up and overtake you,

like a flood of light. Maybe
this is what she means

when she says
she can feel you in the room.

IN LOVE WITH A GIRL EATING STRAWBERRIES

whispering to each
other in the dark

pushing the twin mattress
up against the window

of her tin-can trailer
surrounded by redwoods

and looking up
at the stars—

how the light touches
her body without

going through it. She moves
her hand across my belly

and the pulp in her cuticles
looks like blood

looks like she's reached inside you
to give me something.

But what could I want
from you now? Everything

you could have said
turns to ash inside me.

GOD'S EYE

The kids chase me in the dying light outside the church,
wrapping themselves around my grown body, pulling me down
into the grass. We look up, together this time, and as they press
their small bodies against mine, I want to say something like,
Be good to yourselves, or, *Don't forget this.* And when it's too dark
to see their faces, I become my father, laughing
as he wrestles me off the bed only to pull me back up.
I'm the child kneeling in my mother's chest, looking out as she says,
with her hands on my shoulders, [*Your father's been killed.*]
The night becomes the blanket one of us pulls over the other,
crying ourselves to sleep on the couch. I see the stars, almost
opalescent in the fading sky, and I think of those tiny windows
illuminated outside the basement. I hear my name like an incantation,
like I might forget it otherwise. I see Max standing in the doorway
and I know he knows I'm leaving and not coming back. He rushes into the yard
and grabs my hand, holds it like the last memory of a father, holds it
that close, and drags me inside. If nothing else, let there be more of this.
The tiny rooms filled with light, our awkward and graceless prayers.
You tell me everything and I tell it back without ever looking away.
Grief spilling from your mouth and eyes. How little of it
we've touched, how little of it we'll ever see.

16

[handwritten annotations:]

diagramming sentences of the whole

was/will/can

can/will/is

word/wine/frosty

becoming just

as nostalgic

a what we thought we

were in the past;

like someone in the present

their hearts

saying they can/will

change

past / today / tomorrow

The hustler, gambled dice men of the promise to △

SELF-PORTRAIT WITH SKY LEFT OVER

Pick out the one
and let it stand
for the many—
as sterile
as writing
algebraic formulas
with x=
number of dead
&
and the excel
correlations
between all,
1 and & sea
of all the
different
wars.

who said one versus many of the tragedy

Who believes children anyway? Their bodies
glued together, one afternoon, from scraps of construction paper—

grief and its primary colors
torn to sky in their hands. Or,

All those dead
too many to attempt to
and the pretend
in a moment of silence

maybe my eyes at my father's chest
as he reaches for oranges in the backyard, and if I squint

Instead of Whitman

his arm looks like the hand of god
caressing the face of the sun.

I dream of the souls

Some days I felt so close to nothing
I could have been anything—

the remembrance of whom
and try to
make them proud
& do good

in the fields, tall enough

lifting myself onto the washing machine
in the sunroom, my mother's pale lace

to you

stretched tight over my adolescent hips.
Those afternoons, I learned

Thoughts & Prayers
social media—
the friends of the
the resemble friend who may
have experienced
grief—

look at

The nothingness
of the substitute
as forgotten as
soon as it was
written

being gifted the opportunity to
live the ancestors
& family members you never met

the continues
of pages
thumbing
through the
books as if
it is an album

history &
unfathomable
wars
numbers over names.

to love myself, running
my thumb along the seam

between us. The sky
unfinished, as I stepped into

my body, holding it like prayer
against the window's warm touch.

MEMORIAL

We sat in a circle in the sand
and squeezed your pulse between us.

I closed my eyes. I saw sunlight
drawing the bloody folds of your blue uniform

like waves, the movement of bodies
calling away from themselves.

I felt wind gather itself the way time
accumulates, the airy silences

within each grieving cell. I thought
I was dreaming. I drew a circle in marker

over my heart. I cut a hole from a blue tarp
and stood perfectly still in its center.

I found myself in a body
of water, looking for an edge, instead

finding you everywhere.

ARIZONA

Why now am I thinking about my mother
holding me in the bathtub, afterbirth
floating to the surface of the water, my father's hand

reaching for me, as he sits beside her
on the blue tile floor. How can I imagine this
and not feel the blood moving between us.

Why, after everything has happened
and I stand, watching the fading light soften
the endless canyons before me, do I want to return

to the moment my mother pulls into the driveway,
the crowd of strangers in the blank afternoon,
the policemen who tell her, *Mrs. Dhyne, your husband* . . .

how she dropped to her knees
as a neighbor dragged me across the street,
saying over and over, *He's in a better place now.*

THE WINDOW

The grass caught the light
where it shattered.

I couldn't get back to you.

You, who I wanted to hold
as your heart slowed and opened.

I couldn't put you back together—

picking glass like petals
out of my freckled knuckles.

NEW MEXICO

Tonight the sun drops its bloodstained tongue on the highway. We're driving to Las Cruces, where yesterday somebody put a pipe bomb in the trash and walked away. I wake Jesús in the passenger's seat because I've never seen light that looks like this—like a radiant bruise. Lightning cuts into the sky then disappears. I wonder if we should be afraid. The night's turned black and blue, and my insides feel silver. The lightning in the sky is the blood in my veins. It is the white hand of god flinching at its own power, my father's ghost over my mother's body, a light caress of oblivion. Jesús, I'm afraid—in ten days you fly home to your five sisters and your dying father, your mother who drinks holy water and spits on the car as we leave. But this is how I'll remember you—thin and wild and handsome, hair overgrown and wet with rain, walking through this city's streets at midnight. In ten days, I'll have a new home, and it won't be with you, or in this intersection where lightning has touched in all four directions, and we stand, like in a minefield, holding on to each other. I say your name and look into your eyes. It is your father's name. They are your eyes. Now you say it. The sky flashes once more—this time, a kiss, and you tell me you don't want to die, which means you're thinking about it. Jesús, listen, what if love is waiting for us to annihilate ourselves? It will swallow our voices and we will become a song.

4 A.M.

Where I slip into bed and dream my father's death.
Where the baggage cart that crushed his body

after he hooked it around the concrete pillar, on the tarmac at SFO,
is lifted from his chest and I see him staring up at the sky

as blood pours like honey out of the crushed cave of his sternum.
I can see him as if I were one of those last planes he watched taking off

or a wave of starlings crashing overhead. And because
this is not real, because this is the only way I can explain to you

something I couldn't possibly understand, I can feel his warm blood
pool around my body, I can taste its sweetness.

TEXAS

I don't know where the words come from, but I open
my notebook and there they are. *More blessings than hands.*

Sunset, West Texas. The body remembers being held, and spilling
across hundreds of miles of nothingness, the sun cut by the horizon, light

torn open. *It's only his voice*, my mother said,
holding the tape of my father I never watched.

But I can imagine my one-year-old self reaching for him
behind the camera. If I close my eyes,

he's right there. And when he speaks, the words
dissolve the air between us, as we barrel through god

knows where, Jesús sitting on the window frame as we hit 90
with the wind thrashing his hair. When he looks back

through the windshield, having left his body
in my arms, I turn off the headlights—

we look up at the stars.

A BEGINNING

We light your body on fire. We learn to pray.

Summer opens and falls to its knees. I hold the sun

behind my eyelids. I see your lips on Mom's

swollen belly. She holds your head at both ears.

Listen. I can't go back any further. Look at me

shouting behind the glass, my dumb hands

banging on air. I see you standing on the porch

of the dream. Even here, you're turning

to ash, dissolving into ocean. Years of nothing.

How can I explain this feeling? Mom says

you're still inside me. I trace the lines of my palm

with a switchblade. I learn to beg. I come

over the bathroom sink, drag my palm

across the mirror. Call it horizon. The beginning

of heaven. The house I'm always leaving.

Say, *Goodbye.* I dare you. Say, *I'm sorry.*

My hand reaches for your face. It could fit

in your eye socket, dissolve into night like

your ash on my fingertips. I've forgotten

so much already. I drive across the country.

I fall in love. You have no idea. I look exactly

like you. I dissolve into hands. We smile.

Mom reaches for me across the table, says,

Look how far you've come to get here.

And outside, the rain assembling

like bones in a dream.

LOUISIANA

A man walks by the house and says someone tried
    to burn it to the ground last week, but I tell him we just got here,
we're renting a room for the night. We stumble through

    Bourbon Street, smoking cigarettes, holding beer bottles by the neck,
into a strip club, where a girl named Elizabeth asks me
    if I prefer white girls or black girls and pretty soon

I give her forty dollars and now
    she's on top of me and says I can touch her,
so I do. I place my hands on her small breasts,

    trace my fingers softly across her stomach,
like a child in a gallery. All I want to do is kiss her
    because all I want is for this to be beautiful, and maybe it is

in some fucked-up kind of way, but the truth is
    I can't stand it. I look to my right and Jesús is there
with another girl, riding him with her back turned,

and he gives me this blank, empathetic look
like he has nothing left to give but giving in, and
    I have nothing to say. I look back at Elizabeth and picture her

on a tightrope high above the city. I close my eyes and her body
    pops out of the colorless sky like a bone
pushed through flesh. Everything

    below her is on fire and I don't know
who I'm talking to when I say this,
    but I don't want to be the only one held accountable

for my body. Elizabeth floats off of me with a kiss on my cheek
    and I run to the bar with Jesús. I ask if I can kiss him
and he says *absolutely* and I do.

WITHOUT END

When I finish grieving
my father, my life I think

will begin for real. Safe and warm
in my soft, first shirt.

I try to remember
his touch, but all I feel

is water. The basement flooding,
the bathtub spilling over.

My mother said, *You're lucky,*
you have your father's blood inside you

and I don't. But when Jesús
steps into the shower,

I feel as empty as the water
streaming down our faces.

TENNESSEE

This morning, from a plastic film canister,
we took the two tabs of acid we bought in New Orleans,

called our mothers after pressing them to our tongues,
and wandered past ourselves

into an imagined city, untranslatable
as grief. I thought only our sadness

would outlive us, not these bodies in the landscape,
rearranging under the cruel August sun.

When I say, *We'll have to be each other's mothers,*
it's too late to ask the mirror-light of the river

to forgive us, as our sweat-soaked shirts
begin to cool and we guess our way back

in the dark. Reader, if you believe one thing I tell you,
let it be this. As Jesús sketched my portrait

in the dim light of a rented basement room,
I sat on the floor and wrote, *I'm sorry*

I couldn't be there for you. And yes, I was high
and in love and crying, but I really did feel

my father's spirit move through my body,
that he wrote those words, not me.

LAST WORDS TO MY HUSBAND

Little freckles made of ash,
your ears I cup my lips to—
gone. And yet,

the you I loved is the you I love still.
It swells from the same source—
as one lives (having lived), comes to an ending, then continues

to live. I remember
we made a room of our faces
in the grass. The bridge of our hands sealing

the light between our fingers.
I remember
you asked me to marry you

on a mattress on the floor. I thought I felt you
waking beside me,
dressing in the 4 a.m. glow by touch

alone, and *yes*, I said—
yes. Maybe this is how it feels
when something is taken from a child, replaced with this or that

grief. What we couldn't say
held between us for no other reason but my need
to hold it.

If any part of us stays
it will be these words,
fumbling incoherent radiance

under the door, by the moon,
the beach where you held your camera at your side,
too dark to remember it

this clearly. In a photograph of you
as a child, the sky, overexposed, looks
empty. Who can remember

what goes there now? After our son
drove his fist into the bare white wall of our living room,
he sat there, slouched against it,

head in his hands. The ringing
in his body reaching
for the ringing in mine—

VIRGINIA

We pull to the side of the road
so I can take a piss. In the pouring rain,
at the edge of the field, I look back

and see Jesús in the light
of the passenger's seat mirror.

I remember what my mother said
all summer, as we cleaned out the basement.

I want to feel what it's like
to have openness.

Yet I picture her down there
holding my father's body
on an empty bed frame.

I remember when she told me I'd find love again
even though she might not. *Just imagine*
you're moving toward it.

My mother, whose face flooded with tears,
standing in the doorway my last night
in California, whose pale eyeshadow lit up

radiant with desperation. I want to say,
before everything happens,

I owe her everything.

Two hours from the state line
and the light, when the rain falls,
falls on the field opening before me.

LIKE A GIFT PASSED BETWEEN US

I wanted to ask if you could still imagine his body
    holding yours, your hair sprawled across the pillow like a crown—
but I didn't. I wanted to ask, *Where are you?* or,
    Where are you looking? How your eyes
kept closing toward the other side. How
    I held my body just like his, without knowing.
Mother, what do you remember
    that I am too afraid to ask? For months,
I've been taking the blue pills, halved with a dull blade
    pulled from a desk drawer in the tiny hours of morning.
It has become ritual, like those nights
    where I saw my grief always
as if from a window looking in, our hurried bodies
    slipping between rooms, out of view.
I see the pillows arranged so carefully
    into a circle, I see us lighting the candles
one at a time, saying our names, telling the other families
    how he died. Remember those nights
we held hands over the center console
    driving home, those nights I'd cry out for you,
and that quiet, like a gift passed between us,
    because there was nothing else to give?

How terrible to be at the beginning
    of something ending. As if learning to speak
meant learning how to leave, to disappear
    like a father. *Step into the circle . . .*
if you feel like no one understands what you're going through . . .
    if you still talk to the person you lost . . .
if you're still waiting for them to come back . . .

NOTHING

For years I dreamed of ashes
assembling on the shore

and in the morning
like every morning

his body gone—irrevocable,
like a name, desperate

on a child's tongue. Even the word *father*
continues

to fall away when I speak.
Our desire so far outside ourselves

we might just become it.
This is him, I say, holding the photograph,

window-light catching dust
as it hangs on air.

I once thought the body could disappear
and I was right. And yet—

I can't look at this empty page
without seeing his hands

opening my hands
into light.

I can't think of anything else
when I try to.

There is no other way to say this,
the poem tells me.

If I tell the story in reverse,
it still ends with nothing.

BLACKOUT

I found you
from nearly every angle,
become soft, become
edgeless. Your body
not ash, or water,
or language, but—

Yes. I wanted to say
something about windows
in empty rooms, why we sit
in our two solitudes
not touching. How I can waste
whole days holding your uniform open

to the wind. I remember
nothing of those years, only that I began
hearing myself like music
in the bodies of others. And in the dream,
I saw you moving. But really,
it was the moving I saw, not you.

   //

Hallway: unconscious, out of focus.

I know wherever they took my father looked like this—

a voice sliced open, a scream
I could live in, the child

running toward the horizon
until he runs out of the frame
completely, and the only thing left—
his mother, falling to her knees in the yard

again and again, as if it were some kind
of ceremony, her hands

digging into the earth,
as if they already knew where
to find him, as if she didn't want them
anymore.

Ask me if I want to see
pictures of myself, passed out, somewhere
between what was

and what could have been.
Give me the chance to refuse.

I don't know what happened.

The ambulance lighting up
the far window of my past, a voice
—whose voice?—saying,
Your father was here too.

Did he even have a chance?

Did they look him in the eye
when he called out for me? Did they tear open
his shirt too,

blood-soaked and vacant?
When I wake from my oblivion,
still drunk,

is it my father pushing me out the door
or my mother pulling me close? Mother,
making her bed every night
until she just doesn't care.

How could I have left her?

    //

The word *father*
means nothing now.

Like these lines traced back
into air, my hands

pressed together
as if I could hold them.

What I miss most
is myself, having waited,

given away for so long
whatever I was going to become.

Hear me out:
what I thought meant death

was just one body
telling its story

to the next. We kept
him dead inside us

but that shouldn't really count
for anything, should it?

Otherwise, what am I
wasting my time here for?

I guess what I'm saying
is that I believe

I will see him again.
Our bodies, wet with light.

I believe I have seen it.
The rain,

echolalic. My father,
sitting in darkness

at the edge of his bed,
saying, *Do I feel this unreachable*

to you? If only I could touch
that voice and stand

and walk into the next room.

 //

Where I wrote *light* on the page
I swear I typed your name, your mouth

flickering and ready, like Mother calling
just to hear my voice. Through the door in the dream

you open and fall to your knees. *How are you, then?*
my love asks. The warm reel looping back

around itself, the river of her hair laid out before me,
and in my past I can go anywhere.

I can go anywhere you are.

SELF-PORTRAIT ON THE BELOVED'S BODY

I draw a line from your lips down the center of your chest,
as if to say, *Here is where it happened, here is where grief*

crushed me, where my father's body opened
like a parachute into darkness—

the room with nothing in it, the sound of Mother
crying through the door. I tell you I never wanted to escape

my body. I wanted
to reenter it, to go back to that pain.

My days-old grief (my nine-year-old hands tracing his outline
in the air above my bed.) And when she took us

to see the body, my mother said, *Remember,*
that's not your father—

how can a child understand this?
I lost so many years looking at my own reflection

because I didn't know
where else to find him. Those nights,

my touch was a wasted prayer,
a supplication. All my life, I'd try to explain

and fail. *An accident at work, a spasm of light. No—*
I don't really understand either. But when we touch,

fire asleep in my hand, I realize I am not finished
becoming. Maybe the hour is empty

because it's leaving space for you. My pale torso
glimmering in the halo of light over the bed.

ON SILENCE

When my silence like a fist clutching shards of glass
opens, you ask me what I remember—
a hand on my shoulder and a woman
bending to whisper in my ear.

I am standing in the circle with you. I
squeeze your hand and you squeeze the hand
of the child next to you. We move like this
around the room. You turn and ask me

what I want. Our touch incandescent,
everything opening like a mouth into words.
The mouths of your eyes, the mouths of your lungs—
The mouths of our hearts open like sky and

I have so much to tell you. If this wasn't our story,
it is now. The childhood I never needed to remember,
those empty summers in front of the TV. How I learned
the body's false edges. That we don't end.

95 SOUTH

Busted tires like half-opened birds. That's how you describe them.
$\qquad$ Or maybe you say
$\qquad$ *gutted*, something more beautiful, trace how they fell
$\qquad$ with your finger—
$\qquad$ graceful, idiotic—as we burn through the Georgia coast.
Maybe you name them for your father, everything he could have said
$\qquad$ spilled onto the blacktop.
$\qquad$ You hold your hand to the rusted light, flickering through the pines,
$\qquad$ fold it just above my knee. Who knows
$\qquad$ if this is the one where you take the penknife
$\qquad$ and cut a ring
$\qquad$ around your finger or the one where heaven opens
$\qquad$ and bodies fall from the sky like rags.
Maybe this is the one where I'm already the person
$\qquad$ I've been waiting to become.
$\qquad$ One night at St. Anne's,
$\qquad$ I had the kids make time lines of their lives. They unraveled
fits of yarn in their hands, stitched them wall-to-wall
$\qquad$ over nothing. Like a needle from the other side,
$\qquad$ that feeling I thought
$\qquad$ I'd forgotten. *My dad died today, Left the city, Started fourth grade—*

written on Post-its, pinned to thread. It's one thing to remember, another
    to not forget. A girl says,
            Can I start with my birth? and I ask her if anything happened
                        before that, her eyes bright with wonder.
        We're getting closer
                to St. Cloud, to your father's house.
The sun falls over your side of the car, and I have to squint to look at you
                        as you fold down the mirror,
            drawing the corners of your eyes.
And when you touch your blood-red lipstick to your lips,
        I think of times you've held my father's name in your mouth,
                    how this means you know him as well as I do.
And because this could have ruined me
        but didn't, I want to tell you everything
    so you can remember it for the both of us. How we kept
            switching rooms after he died. How we couldn't stand
to be in the same place, but were too afraid
    to leave. I've written over the memory of that day so many times
                it's night. The first time I slept in the last room
    my father woke up in,
            I heard a moth and its bad wing rip up
            the hardwood floor like a saw.
The door fluttered like an eyelash in a dream,
                and the voice on the other side said,
                        I don't want to leave either.
    Each room in that house remembers me
            differently. I've listened to my mother read my poems
                    to my father in bed,
as if he were there beside her. But sometimes she'd arch her voice

upward, to the attic, where I'd lie on my mattress on the floor,
listening to her mouth my words to him,
back to me.

SONOGRAM

You noticed the pain months ago, imagined
    the polyps, thought to name them
like daughters, that they would have disappeared
    by now. The nurse hands you a towel, and when you return

from the bathroom, placing your feet into the stirrups,
    I feel as though I have been gifted something,
like we have passed through
    a kind of threshold. I hold your bicep, as if

from years away. You lie on the bed,
    not crying, and in the parking lot,
after you've dressed, I assure you there's nothing wrong.
    But what else is there to believe in? If not our pain,

your tears drying on my sunlit shoulder,
    driving home. You say, *Tell me a story*, so I tell you
about your childhood, moving between houses, apartments,
    rooms, beds. What you carry into each, lighter

and lighter and lighter, until I am there and you are here, and then
    we both are. I'm thinking now of this poem,

how you asked me to write it because you couldn't,
    and what I want to say here that I can't say

lying beside you. That I believe
    our bodies are breathing for something else.
That I want to feel like I am you, or as much of you
    as you are, or with you as much as a person can be

with another, meaning,
    we could have felt utterly alone in those minutes.
But isn't it beautiful that these rooms where we leave
    and enter our lives—that it's in these rooms

where we inhabit one another completely,
    as if there was nothing but space for us, meaning
these are not our last bodies, lifted, as if from a box of photographs
    in a child's hands.

PORTRAIT OF MY FATHER AS A YOUNG MAN

You can't be older than seven or eight when I see you smiling
with your mother, leaning against the pillows of two twin beds
pushed together in some tiny apartment in Queens. Your hands are her
    hands,
tangled in movement. The awkward gestures of love, of play.
You don't know what this means to me. The bare white walls of wherever
you are, like the walls of my first apartment with N. Your mother's
head against the pillow, looking up at you, raised slightly above her, and
the beauty here is that you never look away. Your hair buzzed clean,
your big ears, sleeveless undershirt, striped boxers. I want to reach for your
    ankle,
soft and white, wrestle you off the bed, then pull you up again, your hands
reaching for mine. But I shouldn't enter the frame any further.
I know I am not welcome here, but I need to know who is holding
the camera. This feels impossible, that there could be anyone else
on the other side. I can't see what you're holding, and this part is just
    pretend,
but I can almost see you running into the room, out from nothing.
Where were you today, when I wanted to say I missed you?
Salt water seeping through your clothes on the subway, stepping
into the shower alone. Rubbing your hands across the mirror-steam

to see yourself more clearly. That innocent laughter calls us into the other
room. Is this how I was meant to know you? Two lights
glowing at the edges, just out of the frame. Lamp-lit
and warm. Your hands, your bodies—moving.

TELL ME A STORY

And they're crying, holding each other in bed.
I really could have used you when I was younger, he says.

Her hand on his heart, his hand on her cheek.
She leans back against his leg, propped up behind her.

It's not happiness they're feeling but something else,
something they don't have a name for,

recovered. He wants to tell her about his father.
He wants to say, *I wish you could have met him.*

She says, *I hate to think of you as a child, all those years alone.*
And where have they gone to enter into this moment

together? His whole life, her blood almost black
in his cuticles. The hiss of power lines and streetlight

through thin white curtains, the comforter stained
with blood, the blood drying on his thigh, the blood

on her lips. And in the shower, how she shaved his neck
under warm water as he faced away from her,

how it hit their bodies and covered them completely—
the blood now pink, swirling in porcelain at their feet.

She tells him she's afraid of sleeping because
she's afraid of not waking up, so they keep talking

just in case. He shows her pictures of his mother
walking into the ocean with a bag of his father's ashes.

He takes her to meet him, standing on the cliffs,
staring out over the water. *Dad, this is Nichole. Nichole, Dad.*

FATHER'S DAY

In the museum, I press my hand through a square of light
and walk into it. You ask me

if I felt lonely today, and the asking,
more than anything, makes it fall

into place. This quiet clarity now,
like the stillness that comes

the day after rain. Like the recognition
of suffering, or seeing your freckles

as if for the first time. My love,
it's you I'm talking to

when no one is around,
the you my father once was

and sometimes still is. I tell you
I have this memory of looking down at fireworks

from so far above
it can't be real. I tell you this,

and like a dream,
it colors itself in, the sky

pocked with light. I forgot
I had prayed for this,

years ago. I held you as close
as I knew how, running my hands

across my skin. The past tense,
a way of saying

my life sounds so pure
when I tell it back to myself.

It rained the entire drive home through the valley,
but we stopped anyway,

and I took your picture
standing in the middle of the road,

wildflowers blooming on either side of you.

UNTITLED (SAY GOODBYE, CATULLUS, TO THE SHORES OF ASIA MINOR), CY TWOMBLY, 1994

Where there was a meadow,
a shore. Wouldn't that be beautiful, he thought—

to return by sea, which of course implies leaving, or a kind of relief
if we can allow it. And it's true, the beginning of a painting may also be

the beginning of a room. How we followed the canvas toward a door
and there was color there, but no images, as if looking up through glass

from below a great city, the floating roots of a thing we tried to name,
but even then, the words resembled nothing but themselves.

If only we knew how to say *house* and become house, or *gate*
and become gate, we might have the chance to recover—

that I might hear my name and become it. And if I see myself
in a photograph and remember how deeply I have loved and been loved,

if I can hold this past and still take all the hands
out of my poems, the light over the water, the light streaming through

windows, and then not the source of the light itself but only what's lit—
if I could leave the rooms of my past behind and return

to nothing, no body illuminated in waiting—

if I could refuse opening, being opened, at the shore,

at the lips, at my window—what's left?
Who will answer the call of a friend, saying his father is home

from the hospital, on morphine, and barely anything at all?
My being so often shaped into a single moment like this,

curled up on the couch in the dark corner of my apartment
where all I can say is, *I'm sorry, Jesús, I'm so so sorry*, and listen to it ruin you.

But isn't listening its own kind of love?

The stillness of being in time with another, before the world
reenters, and it feels yours again, and impossible.

It's midnight here, which means the sun just left you.
And from where you're sitting on the porch, I can see

the bougainvillea blossoming into the street
where once I stood outside your house and took your picture.

I can see its glowing interior, your sisters moving between rooms,
waiting for him to die. I used to pray for this—

those final moments with my father, his arms around my body
the way a child might hold on to a memory

before it becomes one. Sometimes the image was all I had.
It was so important. It was the saying, the holding on to, the right now

on the floor, something different in the next life kind of knowing.
I am coming to understand this is about me, as I've always hoped
    it wouldn't be—

my name on your tongue, three thousand miles away.
A fucking nightmare, Michael. If only you knew

how to find him after this. *But how will I know?*
How will I know how to do that?

HEAVEN IS EMPTY AND WE'RE ALL IN IT

The empty rooms of my past, empty
    because I needed them to be. But I don't know—

would it have woken you too? Your mother ascending
    out of the dream as she lets go of your hand, saying,
I am going to your father now, I am moving toward him.

    The half-light already awake in your arms, the real tears
on your real face, before you could see where she'd gone.

    And if you asked me what I needed right now,
I couldn't say. If I try to picture my father,
    if I remember him wrong, I wouldn't know the difference.

At any hour of night I come to you
    from a tiny wooden desk with almost nothing on it.

You say you don't remember these moments,
    when you tell me you love me in your sleep,
when you wrap your body around mine.

In death I believe we are a thousand things at once.
We are a body made up of other people's hands.

NOTES

New Mexico:
The final sentence is altered from Marguerite Duras's screenplay for *Hiroshima Mon Amour*.

Without End:
The phrase "Safe and warm in my soft, first shirt" is altered from a line in Jean Valentine's "By the Tekapo River, 100 Degrees."

Blackout:
The final two lines are altered from Jean Valentine's "The Messenger."

Father's Day:
The poem is inspired by James Turrell's *Perfectly Clear (Ganzfeld)*, at the Massachusetts Museum of Contemporary Art.

Heaven Is Empty and We're All in It:
The title is from Tom Andrews's "The Brother's Country."

ACKNOWLEDGMENTS

Thank you to the editors of the following journals where some of these poems first appeared:

The Adroit Journal: "A Beginning" and "Kara"

The Cincinnati Review: "Untitled (Say Goodbye, Catullus, to the Shores of Asia Minor), Cy Twombly, 1994"

The Cortland Review: "Memorial"

Denver Quarterly: "Self-Portrait with Sky Left Over"

Gulf Coast: "Louisiana"

The Iowa Review: "Portrait of My Father as a Young Man"

The Journal: "God's Eye"

Memorious: "Arizona" and "Tennessee"

Nashville Review: "Nothing"

NECK: "Virginia" and "Heaven Is Empty and We're All in It"

Puerto Del Sol: "On Silence" and "95 South"

Raleigh Review("Living Room")

River Styx: "Self-Portrait on the Beloved's Body"

The Rumpus: "Insomnia" and "Blackout"

Salt Hill: "Afterlife"

Smartish Pace: "Last Words to My Husband"

Sonora Review: "New Mexico"

The Spectacle: "Like a Gift Passed Between Us" and "Sonogram"

Washington Square Review: "4 a.m." and "To My Father, the Light"

//

Thank you to my first teachers at the University of California, Santa Cruz, Tim Willcutts, Ronaldo V. Wilson, and Gary Young, for believing I had something worth saying and giving me the permission to say it. This book would not exist without your early encouragement. To my friends Andrew Rosenberg, Dina Marshalek, Karl Smith, and Matthew Francis Brown for being there when I needed you most.

To my teachers at the University of Virginia: Debra Nystrom for guiding this book from the very beginning with tremendous care and insight; Gregory Orr for teaching me how a life-shaping grief can be healed through art; Lisa Russ Spaar for the ecstasy and endless generosity; Paul Guest for your attentive eye; Rita Dove for your wisdom and for teaching us how to dance. To Barbara Moriarty, Jeb Livingood, and Jane Alison for keeping us well-fed and cared for. To my brilliant peers in workshop, especially Valencia Robin, Quinn Gilman-Forlini, Annie Pittman, Courtney Flerlage, and Sean Shearer: your influence is all over these poems. To my students, from whom I learned so much. To Margaret Edwards and the Maxine Platzer Lynn Women's Center for helping me heal many of the wounds this book holds. To Kevin Everson for showing me what light can do.

To the Community of Writers and the Virginia Center for the Creative Arts for the gifts of time and community. To the Bread Loaf Writers' Conference, and the 2019 waiter crew, for making me feel like I belonged. To the friends made along the way: Shelley Wong, Dujie Tahat, Cate Lycurgus.

To Mark Doty for your support and friendship. To Eduardo C. Corral for making this dream come true. To Sean Bishop, Jesse Lee Kercheval, and the wonderful people at the University of Wisconsin Press for ferrying *Afterlife* into the world.

To Jesús Barron for three thousand miles of inspiration.

To Pat Murphy for welcoming me into grief work with immense kindness and generosity. To the families and facilitators at Josie's Place and Kara, the inspiration for so many of these poems. To everyone seeking community in their grief.

To Bobby Elliott, Ollie Brickman, Michaela Cowgill, Rob Shapiro, Landis Grenville, and Ryan Paradiso. Yours are the books that I dream of holding. Let's grow old writing poems together.

To my family, most of all. Jonathan, Mary, Noah, Nani: your love nourishes me everyday. To my father, Jeffrey Dhyne, for your laugh, your curiosity, and for leading me here. To my mother, Barbara Dhyne, for your unending support and encouragement. All that's good in me is thanks to you, Ma. And to Nichole LeFebvre, for this happy, happy life I didn't know was possible.

WISCONSIN POETRY SERIES

Sean Bishop and Jesse Lee Kercheval, series editors

Ronald Wallace, founding series editor

How the End First Showed (B) • D. M. Aderibigbe

New Jersey (B) • Betsy Andrews

Salt (B) • Renée Ashley

(At) Wrist (B) • Tacey M. Atsitty

Horizon Note (B) • Robin Behn

About Crows (FP) • Craig Blais

Mrs. Dumpty (FP) • Chana Bloch

Shopping, or The End of Time (FP) • Emily Bludworth de Barrios

The Declarable Future (4L) • Jennifer Boyden

The Mouths of Grazing Things (B) • Jennifer Boyden

Help Is on the Way (4L) • John Brehm

No Day at the Beach • John Brehm

Sea of Faith (B) • John Brehm

Reunion (FP) • Fleda Brown

Brief Landing on the Earth's Surface (B) • Juanita Brunk

Ejo: Poems, Rwanda, 1991–1994 (FP) • Derick Burleson

Grace Engine • Joshua Burton

The Roof of the Whale Poems (T) • Juan Calzadilla,
    translated by Katherine M. Hedeen and Olivia Lott

Jagged with Love (B) • Susanna Childress

Almost Nothing to Be Scared Of (4L) • David Clewell

(B) = Winner of the Brittingham Prize in Poetry
(FP) = Winner of the Felix Pollak Prize in Poetry
(4L) = Winner of the Four Lakes Prize in Poetry
(T) = Winner of the Wisconsin Prize for Poetry in Translation

The Low End of Higher Things • David Clewell

Now We're Getting Somewhere (FP) • David Clewell

Taken Somehow by Surprise (4L) • David Clewell

Thunderhead • Emily Rose Cole

Borrowed Dress (FP) • Cathy Colman

Dear Terror, Dear Splendor • Melissa Crowe

Places/Everyone (B) • Jim Daniels

Show and Tell • Jim Daniels

Darkroom (B) • Jazzy Danziger

And Her Soul Out of Nothing (B) • Olena Kalytiak Davis

Afterlife (FP) • Michael Dhyne

My Favorite Tyrants (B) • Joanne Diaz

Midwhistle • Dante Di Stefano

Talking to Strangers (B) • Patricia Dobler

Alien Miss • Carlina Duan

The Golden Coin (4L) • Alan Feldman

Immortality (4L) • Alan Feldman

A Sail to Great Island (FP) • Alan Feldman

Psalms • Julia Fiedorczuk, translated by Bill Johnston

The Word We Used for It (B) • Max Garland

A Field Guide to the Heavens (B) • Frank X. Gaspar

The Royal Baker's Daughter (FP) • Barbara Goldberg

Fractures (FP) • Carlos Andrés Gómez

Gloss • Rebecca Hazelton

Funny (FP) • Jennifer Michael Hecht

Queen in Blue • Ambalila Hemsell

The Legend of Light (FP) • Bob Hicok

Sweet Ruin (B) • Tony Hoagland

Late Psalm • Betsy Sholl

Otherwise Unseeable (4L) • Betsy Sholl

Blood Work (FP) • Matthew Siegel

Fruit (4L) • Bruce Snider

The Year We Studied Women (FP) • Bruce Snider

Bird Skin Coat (B) • Angela Sorby

The Sleeve Waves (FP) • Angela Sorby

If the House (B) • Molly Spencer

Wait (B) • Alison Stine

Hive (B) • Christina Stoddard

The Red Virgin: A Poem of Simone Weil (B) • Stephanie Strickland

The Room Where I Was Born (B) • Brian Teare

Fragments in Us: Recent and Earlier Poems (FP) • Dennis Trudell

Girl's Guide to Leaving • Laura Villareal

The Apollonia Poems (4L) • Judith Vollmer

Level Green (B) • Judith Vollmer

Reactor • Judith Vollmer

The Sound Boat: New and Selected Poems (4L) • Judith Vollmer

Voodoo Inverso (FP) • Mark Wagenaar

Hot Popsicles • Charles Harper Webb

Liver (FP) • Charles Harper Webb

The Blue Hour (B) • Jennifer Whitaker

American Sex Tape (B) • Jameka Williams

Centaur (B) • Greg Wrenn

Pocket Sundial (B) • Lisa Zeidner